Optimize Your Sales Closings

Learn the skills that will make you money and increase your closings by up to 70%

Akia Taylor

For information contact:

Optimize Your Spark Inc.
Phone: 917-426-4611
Email: Akia@AkiaTaylor.com
http://www.OptimizeYourSpark.com

Book and Cover Design: by Refinery 9 Inc.
Content Editor: Anita Webster
Author Photograph: Taylor Studios

First Edition: June 2017

10 9 8 7 6 5 4 3 2 1

"BEHIND EVERY SALE IS A NEED."

Akia Taylor

Dedicated to Francisco Liriano
Rest in peace.

TABLE OF CONTENTS

FOREWARD

SELLING IS TRULY AN ART FORM. Not everyone is good at selling and most people are afraid of what selling really means. Selling requires a person to think outside of herself and that's uncomfortable. But, it doesn't have to be.

In Optimize Your Sales Closings, author Akia Taylor, is speaking to the novice sales leader and to the seasoned sales person, alike. She carefully helps the reader understand how selling works so you can enhance your selling skills, masterfully. Beginning with a keen understanding of the role mindset plays in your ability to sell, Akia shares stories and real-world examples of selling success. Yes, you must understand you own beliefs about money and "fix" them in order to step into successful sales conversations.

The opportunities are clear. You just have to pay attention and apply what you learn to make the difference in your business. As a trained, NLP professional, I love the transparency and intention behind all of the robust lessons Akia includes in the chapters. She's studied and applied NLP. It shows and she readily shows you how to learn from her experiences.

Prepare yourself to close more sales using a very, strategic and conversational approach. Akia gives you the tools to make it happen. I especially appreciate the suggestions she offers about asking questions to address objections before they occur. This is the work of an NLP master that typically requires years of training and practice. Akia lays it all out purposefully for you the reader to understand.

If you're not great at selling, after reading Optimize Your Sales Closings, you will be. It partners the tools with the strategy to help you understand buying behavior and signals, as well as, what you say "next" to complete the transaction and close the sale. Break out your highlighter and prepare to immerse yourself in study so you can become the masterful sales leader necessary to thrive in your business.

Wendyy Bailey
Master Business and Sales Coach, CEC, C.NLP
Income Acceleration Mentor at Business Beyond Limit

PREFACE

EVERY CONVERSATION THAT YOU HAVE is an energy exchange and an exchange of ideas. You have your point of view on things and I have a point of view too. As you trade ideas and points of view you are engaged in a sale of new and sometimes different points of view.

As a business owner, you need to become a sales pro in order to seal the deal with your potential clients as well as with your existing ones. Since sales has gained a not-so-great reputation, it really takes skill to a close sale without making your client (the buyer) become uncomfortable. So, from a very genuine place, you will use conversational sales skills in order to get your client out of their own way and to buy. It is human nature to avoid making decisions that are not seen as pressing in nature or are uncomfortable. You will use discomfort to motivate.

Even still, a lot of times sales professionals are concerned about coming off as a sleazy salesman. What you may not realize is that the idea behind what makes a sales professional sleazy is not THAT they are selling, but HOW.

When sales professionals come off like all they care about is the sale it creates mistrust and unease in your buyer. However, when you create a consultative and conversational space, it will feel differently to your buyer.

Remember, consultative selling allows for an exchange of ideas and of energy as you move with your buyer towards a common goal. It helps your buyer to feel as though you, as their sales person, is working with them and not on them. This will allow you to easily gather enough information about them and their situation to avoid objections before they arise. If/ when objections DO arise, you will use this information to help your buyers buy.

Sales professionals provide solutions. All barriers in your sales conversations stand in the way of your buyer and their solution. In this book, we will learn how to navigate the process of conversational sales skillfully.

Who is Akia Taylor?

I AM NEW YORK NATIVE born in the concrete jungle. I was raised in the Bronx and am the product of a single parent household. I am the youngest of four children. (YEAH, YEAH...I'm the baby)

I spent most of my educational years in private school. At age eleven when my standardized tests results came in and I was scoring off the charts in genius territory my future looked bright. But after high school, money concerns were real and college was not in the cards for me. With some negotiation, I ended up in a community college and decided it was time to go to work.

I got my first REAL job in a large commercial bank behind the teller window. I knew within two months that I did not want to be there for long. (The disrespect that customer service professionals endure is immense.) I approached the branch manager and spilled my guts. I shared how unhappy I was and asked what the secret sauce was to getting from behind that window and getting a promotion into management. He said, "Sell." And so, that is what I did. With little sales training, I began closing deals. I spoke with every customer that visited my window. I found my selling style. With time, I actually became good at it. Within 6 months of the start of my banking career, I was promoted into management.

I was fortunate to work with some of the most pioneering sales professionals in the bank. My then mentor, Francisco Liriano, launched a sales outreach "Bank-at-work" program that the bank still uses to this day. Guess who was right by his side. This girl. (Franciso lost his life on the 105th floor of Tower 2 in the World Trade Center on the day we will never forget 9.11.2001) This book is dedicated to him. He is the person the lit the passion for sales within me.

I used those sales skills and made my way right on up that corporate ladder. I eventually became a stock broker near

New York City's Wall Street for another major commercial banking institution. If you know anything about being a stock broker, possibly from watching some of those great movies on it, you will know that I really had to step my sales closing game up at that point.

Somewhere around 9/11 when the world was changing, I realized that banking was not the industry fo me (If you are doing your math right, you will quickly realize that sales knowledge was gained OVER 15 years.) I, along with the rest of the world, decided to try my hand at technology. I made the move to see how I was in tech. support and not long afterward moved into technology sales, of course. It was at this time I began learning more about marketing, products, branding, visibility and placements. I learned at the feet of some of the most powerful, most influential and the most successful companies of our time including Google, Apple, and Microsoft. While working with Google I was the top Chrome sales representative in NYC as well as one of the top sales representatives in Microsoft retail for NYC. It was at this time I realized I was onto something.

I also had this special talent. I had a knack for business. My friends and family realized it too. I had supported them a for about a decade as they started businesses and provided direction that was empowering, insightful, supportive and LUCRATIVE.

Finally, in January 2015, I decided to pull all of my experience, education, innate ability, and expertise together. I didn't realize what I had been doing all this time was called "coaching" up to that point. When I identified that this was a THING I began studying my craft and am now a Certified Business Coach. I am also a Certified Master NLP Practitioner and a Certified NLP Sales Trainer. As a result of wanting to teach and train, I am also a Sales Speaker. (I think things came together rather nicely.)

My passion for helping people like you to win in their business is what has gotten us here to this point. Inside these pages, I will share with you what I have learned, tested, perfected and employ in order to help YOU to your win in your business.

ACKNOWLEDGEMENTS

Where would I be without my Lord and Savior? I am grateful Father for your mercy and for keeping the path lit.

To Mommie, thank you for doing the best you could. I am the woman I am today because of your love

To Rod, you changed my life. I do not know how I lived before you.

To Brooke, you make me a better person. I strive to be better and better because I know that you are watching.

To Kim, I love you sis. Thank you.

To Arthur, I appreciate you baby.

INTRODUCTION

ONCE YOU GET PAST THE MUSHY, star-gazed, I will take over the world feeling in your business, you will quickly realize that you need a great engine to go under the hood and to power your vehicle when you decide to be successful.

This book is the engine under your hood. Conversational sales conversations will allow you to create opportunities in your business and will make your vehicle (your business) a strong one. In addition to the tangible benefits of strong closings, (money) there are many intangible benefits as well. They not only influence your bottom line but they also influence how your clients see your business in general. (confidence and trust)

Successful and strong sales conversations have several key components. I have narrowed this process down for you into 10 steps. As a result, I have created a genuinely heartfelt but absolutely KICK ASS series of tools and programs designed to help you increase your sales closings by up to 70% and master your money.

Having the use of my experience and of the resources I will provide you here will allow you to:

- Be a skilled sales leader
- Establish yourself as the expert
- Establish value in your product
- Generate more sales(wealth) in your business
- Take your business in the direction of growth
- Get clear on your goals
- Decide how to meet your goals
- Deepen relationships with your clients
- Create appeal in your offers for your clients
- Establish confidence both personally and professionally

These tools will allow you to provide your buyers and potential clients with solutions that will help them to go from hesitant skeptics that have an unfulfilled need to absolutely sold and fans that are also your clients.

MINDSET

BONUS

Where it all begins

THE MINDSET OF A SALES PROFESSIONAL influencer and thought leader is one of a person preparing for a win.

As we move through this life we gain experience by the ton and if we are lucky, we learn from those experiences quite a bit. Some of the experiences are wonderful while others, not so much. Whether the experience is up or down, they shape how we move through life as well as who we are as people. Some of those things change or belief systems as well.

EXAMPLE:

> *If your parents are like mine, they worked for corporate America every day until retirement. As a result, you watched your parents and learned that this is how responsible adults behave. If your parents believed that the only way people acquire money and stability was to work 9-5 for someone else they would teach you the same. You would learn that THIS is what hard work and adult responsibility looked like. You would grow and make decisions from this place. The only way to make money is in the same way you were taught.....like your parents did!*

If /when you began taking the steps to create your own business this will go against what you have watched and have been taught. This step will inherently have limiting beliefs. A limiting belief is a belief that imposes a glass ceiling in your mind. There are usually subconscious barriers. Not ones that we are even aware exist. They are also mostly not based in fact. Some of the limits may not even be real at all.

You will engage in self-sabotaging activities or behaviors as a result of limiting beliefs when you begin to venture outside of that limit. This may actually reinforce the limit and provide false evidence that the belief is true.

EXAMPLE:

> *For many years, my salary hovered around 42K-46K. Somewhere in my mind, I sought out opportunities in that salary range. I subconsciously believed that was what my skill set was worth. I limited myself to the opportunities that fit this idea that I created about*

myself. If an opportunity came about that paid more, I would feel anxious that I was getting in over my head. I became my own worse enemy and created a money block.

This lack of confidence in your abilities and ultimately in yourself spill out into your sales conversations. Oddly enough, you will feel the hole is in your CLIENTS' confidence or in their ability to pay or is a deficit in their ability to see value in your offer. In fact, this may really be all you! This problem may actually just be a lack of confidence ...in yourself. It is more likely a reflection of your inability to see your own value and of that in your offer than it is a reflection of your client.

Why are you doing that?

The answer is simple. It is easier for you to see holes or deficits in your client. It is easier to swallow that your client may have an inability to see your value than it is to admit or even acknowledge that you can't see value in yourself. But this relationship is a reciprocal one. In truth, they may not be able to fully see our value because you are not sure of it in yourself.

So....we gotta fix that. These issues show up in your business and block your ability to get money. A money block. This is where your work comes in. To be honest, this may be the most challenging, yet the most freeing part of closing sales. This is the part where you deal with you. I can guarantee with 100% certainty that you will not see the results that you want to in your business until you overcome this. You will find ways to sabotage yourself and subsequently your results until you do.

Money Beliefs Worksheet

GET A SHEET OF PAPER AND ANSWER THE FOLLOWING:

1. What are your beliefs about money?

2. What are your beliefs about how you acquire money?

3. Where did those beliefs come from?

4. What are your ideas around your worth?

5. Where did those ideas come from?

6. What are your thoughts on the value of the product or service you provide?

7. How can you overcome any negative feelings you've identified?

8. How can you expand any positive feelings you have identified?

9. How can you bring your positive feelings into your sales conversations?

10. Have your feelings about value and worth changed? How so?

11. How do you plan to consistently sell from this more positive space?

TABOO WORDS

THERE ARE WORDS TO AVOID when engaged in a sales conversation.

Before you begin selling you need to be aware of the language that you use to do so. This is my FAVORITE part of this whole learning experience. It was insightful for me as I took a look at the words I choose to use on a regular basis as part of my everyday vocabulary. I had no idea that I had been adding negative energy or negative emotion to my conversations. That said, this part of the training is useful in everyday life.

There is a psychology to sales conversations. For those of you who have studied NLP like I have, you know there is power in all words and conversations. The power of words is immense! You can cause a person to feel emotional, rational, warm, cold, become your friend or make a terrible enemy only by using your words. In the Bible, the Lord created the world that we live in today with His words. He created you and me with His words. Now that is power. Words have **POWER!**

Taboo Words are words that we should avoid in our sales conversation for several reasons:

1. They cause people to feel put off by us.

2. They cause a distraction in your conversation. (Consequently, letting the fish off the hook)

3. They introduce negative language into your sales conversation.

4. When you begin speaking negativity into your sales conversations your buyer will follow your lead.

When you are working face-to-face in a sales conversation with a buyer you can read as well as control you buyer, with body language. You are mostly looking for negative positions or guarded body. Guarded body language is an indication of how your buyer is receiving you. It looks like folded arms, crossed legs, closed hands,...etc. Conversely, open body language looks like hands with palms up, sitting up in their seat with the buyer leaning into you or towards you. The difference between the two is that open body language creates no visual barriers between you and your buyer where closed body language does. You can encourage or discourage this by exhibiting open body language yourself. You buyer will mirror you.

Taboo Words are the equivalent of closed body language in your sales conversation with your buyer. They create a barrier between you and your buyer. There are words that we should use instead of Taboo Words called Enticing Words. Enticing Words invoke more of a positive feeling in your sales conversation. Again, words have power. In this instance, they have the power to persuade your buyer either way. It is your job as the sales professional to leave a favorable impression on your buyer so that they will buy.

Here is a list of Taboo Words:

- Honestly
- Contract
- Buy
- Problem
- Prospects
- Cheap
- Cost
- Perhaps
- Guarantee
- Discount
- Sign/ signature
- Commission
- Pitch
- Customers
- Advice

- Hope
- Don't/Can't/Won't
- Obviously
- Quota
- Maybe
- Cheaper
- Competitor
- Price
- Forbidden
- Objections
- Free
- No

You should also avoid speaking poorly about vendors/merchants/service providers offering similar support. This can make your buyer feel uncomfortable and change the way they view and respect you as a professional.

ENTICING
WORDS

WORDS THAT YOU SHOULD SAY when engaged in a sales conversation to create positivity.

In the same way, you can create negative emotion you can also create positive emotion in a sales conversation and influence the buyer's buying decision positively. To buy or not is an emotional decision. Think about it. You buy from your favorite places and people all the time. The fact that these places and people made it to your favorite list was not through a logical decision, but an emotional one. You like them because...well...you like them. This is why your buyers will buy from YOU as well. Using Enticing Words will encourage this with your buyer and will end in great rapport, trust, and a sale.

Here is a list of Enticing Words:

- Agreement
- Purchase
- Concern
- Clients
- Inexpensive
- Investment
- Definitely
- Reduced price
- John Hancock
- Reward
- Offer

- Suggestion
- Certain
- You may have noticed
- Goal
- Less expensive
- Similar market
- Discouraged
- Concern
- Complimentary
- Value

Say instead:

Benefits vs. Specifications
Learn vs. Show
Emotion vs. Reason
You vs. I

One of the most persuasive words in the English language (it is in the top 5) is the word "because." The word because instantly answers the question "what is in it for me "from your buyer.

EXAMPLE:

> If while you were in line waiting to order your favorite coffee or latte a guy rushes into the store, looks down the line, gets frustrated and then jumps the line in front of you, you would be angry.

However, if while you were in line waiting to order your favorite coffee or latte a guy rushes into the store, looks down the line, gets frustrated and makes eye contact with you. He says" Miss, I am running late to work! I am supposed to bring my boss his favorite latte every day but today my car broke down. I am running late BECAUSE I took the train today rather than drive. I need to get in front of you so I won't get fired!

Notice, I did not ask permission, which is still rude. HOWEVER, the use of the word because mixed in with his story at least make you consider his situation making his jumping the line a bit more platable, even though you may still say no.

When quoting prices to your clients there is always the fear that they will experience sticker shock. To avoid this, position your offer so that it is easier to swallow. (You can say just about ANYTHING if you position it properly) Since you want to help your buyer overcome barriers and obstacles in order to relieve pain points and purchase relief through you, it is important that you quote your prices in a way that doesn't scare people away. When quoting prices avoid saying two THOUSAND NINE HUNDRED DOLLARS. Instead, say twenty-nine hundred or twenty-nine ninety-seven. Quoting prices this way makes then sound less intimidating. Making your prices sound less intimidating will help you to avoid a price objection.

YOUR GREETING

SET UP YOUR CLOSING FROM the very beginning by creating rapport and trust with your greeting.

Be sure that your physical appearance supports your brand and conveys a message that you want to leave your buyer with. People will begin judging you from the moment that you walk into a room. (Human beings have had to make quick assessments of situations since the beginning of time. Once-upon-a-time, our safety and survival depended on it.) Immediately, people will begin sizing you up. You want to ensure that they have the tools they will need in order to make the correct initial assessment of you.

Are you not you guilty of doing this yourself? (Uh...I am. When I meet a new person or ANY person really, I am checking them out fully...100% of the time.) Avoid wearing the wrong colors to an event with people who represent certain colors or wearing something inappropriate. (i.e. Wearing a low-cut blouse in front of certain religious groups or wearing red to speak at a school whose colors are blue but their rivals wear red.) You can instantly discredit yourself or shoot yourself in the foot with a distraction before you even open your mouth.

1. Introduce yourself.

This creates an instant bond with your buyer and offers a small piece of familiarity. After an introduction, we are no longer strangers. There is now a level of respect (albeit minor) between you and your buyer.

A great thing to include in your introduction besides your name is your title and what you do (as it pertains to your buyer) What you want them to know is that they are in good hands with you. "I am not new to this." This information establishes trust and will help your buyer to understand why listening to you is a good idea. You will help them deduce "she must know what she is talking about." And, you do!

Now that you have provided your name, title and what you do, give them a little background information about yourself. This will further explain why they should listen to and trust you. You will gain instant creditability and respect. You will begin positioning yourself as the subject matter expert or the SME. People are going to respect and value the advice acquired from an expert.

EXAMPLE:
- My name is Akia Taylor. (Who I am.)

- I am a Certified Business Coach and a Marketing and Sales Trainer. (What I do.)

- I have worked in marketing and sales for 20 years. I have been fortunate enough to work with several major corporations including Citibank, JPMorgan Chase, Apple, Google, Microsoft, and Volkswagen. I have learned a great deal working with some of the greatest corporations of our time.

2. **Well-placed talking points.**

A lot of times in sales conversations we put pressure on ourselves to get our whole message in there. To your buyer, this method comes off as overwhelming and as too much information, even if it isn't. A person can only take in but so much information (even if it isn't really a whole lot) and process it. Manage your information sharing so that you do not overwhelm your buyer.

Manage your pace. Often (again, because you are trying to get it all in and as a result of that pressure we just mentioned) speaking quickly is a common mistake among sales professionals. Your buyer needs to process the information that you are presenting. If they perceive that you are speaking quickly, they may feel that you are trying to get something over on them. Like you are literally trying to get something past them. (Remember, a person's preception is their reality. Whether it is true or not a person's perception is their truth.) No one likes a fast-talking salesperson.

✳✳✳

When you speak quickly in your sales conversations and neglect to control your pace your buyer may perceive fear or lack of confidence from you. When a buyer senses this, they may begin attempts to take over a conversation. Or they may lose confidence in you and tune you out altogether. Both equal no sale for you and absolutely should be avoided.

***

A trick that I employ in my sales conversations in order to help me pace myself and to ensure that I am on the same page as my buyer is to ask questions. I ask check-in kinds of questions of my buyer like "Does that sound good" and "Does that make sense?" Checking in with your buyer is always a smart move. This allows your buyer the opportunity to share and to be heard by you. This is a great way to draw out objections so that you don't have them pop up on you later while attempting to close. It gives a nice break fro YOU talking

3. No matter what your buyer says, stay positive.

There will be times that you will work with someone who is skeptical or a tough pill as we affectionately call them. Long story short, some buyers will test you. Other buyers are looking for you to give them a reason not to buy. Once you return a buyer's negativity you give them permission to continue to be negative. This can be perceived as a form of escalation and rather incendiary.

Instead of returning negativity, remain positive and upbeat. Believe it or not, this is another type of sale. Either your buyer will sell you on their terrible outlook or you will sell them on your positive one. I can tell you which one ends in a closed sale!

Next, you will identify who is making the buying decision for the purpose of a successful close.

FINDING THE DECISION MAKER

AVOID AN OBJECTION LATER by selling to the right buyer from the very beginning.

There are clues that you miss in sales conversations that cost you your sale. In every instance, if you recognized the clues and utilized the opportunity to apply some skill, those pop-up objections could be avoided. They can, literally, be moved out of the way before they threaten the closing of your sale. AND, they are not so pop-up.

The art of finding the decision maker is something you must do at the very beginning of a sales conversation. It is the key to helping you avoid a sales objection later. (Although we will speak in greater detail about sales objections in later chapters, every sales professional has had a sale derailed by one. If you have had a sale derailed by an objection I am sure you are game to get away from lines like, "I need to ask my husband" or "I am just looking at some options for my friends/family." You can avoid both with the proper skill set.) Remember, it is best to get this potential derailment out of the way fairly early in your sales conversation. When you execute your sales conversations in the same conversational manner that you do your regular conversations, you will gain valuable knowledge without your buyer knowing that you are information gathering. In my experience, several variations of the following questions can be asked to help you determine whether or not you are in front of your buyer or who the buyer truly is.

Questions like:
- What brings you here?

- Who is the product/service for?

- How will you be using it?

- Is someone else making this purchase with you?

***

If you discover that there are others responsible for the buying decision or that the decision is shared, you will then need to determine how to introduce the other party to your sales conversation. Some sales professionals ask that the decision maker is included by phone call or some other conference. No matter the method, the goal is to be sure that all the decision makers get the information they will need in order to make a favorable decision. (When you discover that you are not speaking with the decision maker your focus should now shift to making contact with them and bringing them up to speed.)

If you are unable to get to the decision maker and think that your buyer is throwing them into the conversation in a smoke and mirrors attempt, you can gather information about them for use later on in your conversation when an objection arises.

EXAMPLE:

- "Based on what you shared about your wife, I know that this is a great choice. One you/she will enjoy."

- "Your wife sounds a lot like me. I would love it if my husband did something like this for me!"

You can always add some information about a money back guarantee or your refund policy to create ease and trust. Be sure to include that you know that they will not need it as they have invested in a great option.

The lesson here is that ignoring the decision maker, whether they are present or not, is a mistake. Once you get this settled you will move into setting the agenda of your sales conversation for your buyer.

SETTING THE AGENDA

ESTABLISH TRUST AND PROFESSIONALISM by setting the agenda of your conversation for your buyer.

By this time, you have established rapport with your buyer. You have provided them with information with regard to who you are and what you do. You have also gathered some information from your buyer at this point too. You should have enough information to determine what brought them here and what they are looking for from you. You may have even discovered the pain point that they are trying to relieve with your product or service. (Human beings function better in an environment that lends itself to order and control. It is difficult to be relaxed and trusting when you aren't sure of what is expected of you or what comes next, right? A doctor's bedside manner is a great example of our next step.)

You, the salesperson, will provide order and control for your buyer by setting the agenda for your conversation and helping them to feel comfortable about what is coming next. It is a gesture towards collaboration and suggests a couple things to your buyer. Prior to setting the agenda, you will need to do a couple of things.

1. Always ask permission to proceed with your line of questions before you proceed with them. When you engage in a question exchange with your buyer, be sure that the exchange does not feel like the French Inquisition to them. **(uh...do not be creepy)**

   Try something like, "Is it ok if I ask a few questions in order to get a better understanding of where and how I can support you?" (They will not say no, I promise. How would that work out for them anyway???) "Um...no. You cannot ask me anything because although I am here with you seeking help I really do not want you to help me." (Not likely huh? Notice that the question I asked ends with a yes. This is done because we want to get the buyer saying yes from the very beginning.)

2. Probe to uncover pain points. You need to sell to the WIFM or the "what is in this for me", for your buyer ultimately. Your buyer is looking to relieve some point of discomfort. You will need to include that point on the agenda to explain or illustrate how you will relieve it and to remind your buyer that it exists so that they WANT you to relieve it. This step also allows your client to see that relieving that pain point for them is your main focus. They have a friend in you. That is what is in it for them...no more discomfort.

***

You will then assimilate all the information that you have gathered and then present the agenda for your conversation which ultimately will be to relieve your client of that pain point you found. Your agenda presentation should sound like this:

EXAMPLE:

> "Thank you for allowing me to gather some information from you and for freely sharing. I hate that you are struggling with ......(insert pain point here) I can help. I will discuss my product/service with you because it will help you to overcome your pain point by helping you to:
>
> 1. Acknowledge that that pain point exists.
>
> 2. Gain the tools needed to overcome the pain point.
>
> 3. Posses the product or service that will help you to not have to experience that pain point again.

Follow ALL that up with "Does that sound good?" (This is a way of asking permission to proceed with the conversation and making sure you and your buyer are on the same page. Notice the YES question. Remember to keep you buyer saying yes.)"

When you set the agenda for your buyer, you provide a level of control and establish yourself as the SME. (subject matter expert) your buyer will value you and your suggestions in this position. Next. you will use questions to gain more control of your sales conversation and to move the buyer in the direction that you intend for them to go. The moment you lose control of your sales conversation is the same moment you lose your sale.

LEARNING NEEDS

ASKING QUESTIONS IS THE WAY to learn all you need to about your buyer.

There is an art to asking questions in a conversational way. Doing so is important because no one wants to be on the wrong end of an interrogation. The consideration here is to remember to not be so consumed by the sale that you forget to move through the sale like a human being and not like a wolf! You must create a conversation to avoid awkward, rapid-fire questioning.

In order to open conversation, discover pain points and information gather you will need to ask:

- Open-ended questions

- Close-ended questions

- Transitional questions

1. **Open-ended questions** are questions that will lead to an open dialog. In order to open up your conversational sale, you will need to ask open-ended questions to encourage broad responses in your attempt to information gather. Open-ended questions should be asked with an agenda and not randomly. There is no telling where the answer to an open-ended question may lead.

Examples of open-ended questions are:
- How are you?

- What benefit are you hoping to gain from this product or service?

- What other open-ended questions might you ask of your buyer in an effort to gather information from them?

Open-ended questions can end with your buyer going off on tangents. It is important that you discourage this by not going off on a tangent yourself.

2. **Close-ended questions** are questions with a definitive closed answer; yes or no. For this reason, these questions are used mostly toward the end of your sales conversations in an effort to gain agreement from your buyer. They should be used by you, a skilled sales person, to get your buyer into the habit of telling you yes. If there is a chance that the answer to your close-ended question is no, don't ask it. (Muy importante!)

Examples of close-ended questions are:

- Would you like to close more sales?

- Would you like to make more money?

- Can you image yourself being free of the pain point we just discussed?

What other close-ended questions can you ask in order to get your buyer telling you "YES?"

3. **Transitional questions** are questions used to go from topic to topic. They are also used to gain or to maintain control of your sales conversation. When used with a talkative buyer they will keep your conversation on track and moving towards a close. Transitional questions usually follow open-ended ones because open-ended questions are so broad in nature. It is VERY easy for your buyer to get off track there. When they do, it is transitional question time. Transitional questions are also mostly close-ended yes or no questions. This will allow you to narrow the conversation down and get it back on track.

Examples of transitional questions are:
- I am sorry to hear that you are not having such a great day. Our discussing how to ease your pain point should make it go better, right?

- My household supports small business owners too. Isn't it a great feeling to be able to do that AND get the services you need too?

- I am glad to hear that you are accomplishing the goals you set for yourself for your 2018. Doesn't that feel good? (transitional, close-ended) What do you have planned next and how can I help? (open-ended)

The learning needs part of your conversation is very important to closing your sale. While doing so, remember that buyers are said not to care about what you know until they know that you care. The buyer needs you to show interest in them over you showing interest in closing the sale. Remember this as you move through your conversation but in this section especially.

You will use the information gathered in this part of your conversation in order to remind your buyer why they are in front of you and of how you can help them overcome the problem that brought them to you. (Sales professionals refer to this as uncovering the pain point. You will use this to information to overcome objections.) Once you discover why the buyer is in front of you need to make the hole they are attempting to fill bigger. And bigger. And BIGGER than life! You need to make the hole as big as possible by allowing you buyer to feel the discomfort of their pain point. Then, superhero, sales professional YOU comes in to save the day for your buyer with your product/service as you fill the hole, satisfy the need and relieve your buyer.

Next, you will use what you've gathered in order to deliver value
BUT...it all starts with questions.

DELIVERING VALUE

THE TIME HAS COME for you to show off your service or product to your buyer.

This is the opportunity for you to show off your wares. Your buyer has begun opening up to you. They have shared what is troubling them and they have brought their troubles to YOU. Now, you will begin to fill in the gaps.

1. The first thing you want to do here is to restate the buyer's pain point for a couple different reasons.

   A. You want to show your buyer that you heard them and that you are both on the same page.

    B. To expand the hole created by re-introducing (serving a reminder) their pain point... that you are preparing to fill.

    C. After you have restated the problem, you will gain agreement on their pain point to be sure that you are working to solve the right problem. (Doing this reinforces that you were listening to your buyer yet again. It reinforces trust in your new relationship because you are now speaking the same language.)

2. Deliver your solution to their pain point. In order to deliver your buyer's solution, you have to clearly sell to the WIFM (what is in it for me) for your buyer. Not meaning what is in it for YOU but what is in it for THEM. The best way to deliver these solutions is to do it through presenting features and benefits followed by a value statement.

Features explain what the product or sevrice has to offer. The details of it; the specifications. Benefits explain how the product or service will satisfy the pain points you discovered of your buyer. There are different schools of thought regarding which you should lead with, features or benefits, in your sales conversations. I tend to blend the two but I LEAD with benefits and the reason is this. Benefits sell. Since they soothe pain points and pain is what your buyer wants to get away from, the benefits of a product or service is what your buyer is really here for.

3. Deliver your value statement by relating everything back to your buyer's need after presenting their benefits and

features in the form of a presentation. (Your buyer will automatically relate some of the benefits you presented to themselves organically.) When you deliver your value statement you can clearly illustrate to your buyer where they are in your solution. It is all about them. You will illustrate to them how you will help them fix it and where YOUR value lies in the equation.

You have gained the trust of your buyer and have worked up to the point that you can deliver your value statement. You have worked to build rapport, gain trust and to be seen as the expert. By this time your buyer will understand that you have more knowledge than most others or at least more knowledge than they do on this subject. You will deliver your expert statement in that vein. Your expert statement can begin like this: "I recommend..."

Help your buyer trust your judgment by following up your value statement with the word "because." Begin explaining why you have taken this position on what their next steps should be. Why is this their best choice? You always gain more trust when you explain why. You are finally armed with the information you need and will use to close successfully and to get paid!

OVERCOMING SALES OBJECTIONS

SALES OBJECTIONS ARE BARRIERS RAISED by your buyer in an attempt not to buy.

More often than not, although your buyer is uncomfortable in their current position, they have become comfortable being uncomfortable....if that makes sense. Discomfort and pain points are not a sure shot that you will avoid a sales objection.

In truth, if you have followed the steps that I have provided for you up to this point, you should have already drawn out the large majority of your buyer's possible objections. (Objections can largely be avoided by thoroughly exploring in the "Learning

Needs" part of the sales conversation when you continue to probe or ask questions of your buyer. This must be done in a conversational way, of course over in an interrogative way.) Sales professionals agree that the moment the first objection is raised is that same moment that the REAL selling begins.

Overcoming objections requires that you really listen to what your buyer is saying. You should always repeat the objection presented in an effort to demonstrate to your buyer that you are paying attention. After you repeat and gain agreement on what the buyer's concern is you will overcome the objection(s) by employing skill.

1. One of the popular ways sales leaders actually overcome objections is to use the information gathered in the "Learning Needs" part of your conversation. You will have to give them back what they gave you to remind them of why they came to you in the first place. (The pain points.) You have to expand the pain points to an unbearable place. By bringing the buyer back to this place, you will demonstrate the importance of taking action by closing the sale with you.

2. Sales professionals will also overcome objections by painting a picture fo their buyer of a world without the pain.

3. Another method used by sales professionals to overcome objections is identifying which type of buyer they are working with in order to smoothly move the conversation from sales objections to a solid closing. This method requires that you, the sales professional, plays close

attention so that you can classify your buyer correctly and ensure the proper closing and subsequently make CASH!!

Here are the four types of buyers

- The indecisive buyer

- The knowledgable buyer (dominant)

- The easy-going buyer

- The skeptical buyer

Which type of buyer are you?

Let's talk briefly about what an objection is not. An objection is not a question. When your buyer has questions at this stage, it is a strong indication of interest. This is called a buying cue. Buying cues are hints that your buyer is weighing this decision and is preparing to buy. Be patient through the questions. Once you get them out of the way to your buyer's satisfaction, you are ready to close.

TYPES OF SALES CLOSINGS

THERE ARE FOUR TYPES of buyers that you will encounter in your sales conversations.

As a sales professional, you will increase your odds of successfully closing when you know what type of buyer you are engaging. This will also allow you to employ the most effective closing for each buyer. Becoming a master at this will allow you to be more effective at closing and at generating more revenue.

In this chapter, we will learn about the different types of buyers. And then, we will learn how to close each buyer in the most skillful way.

Here are the four types of buyers:
- The indecisive buyer

- The knowledgable buyer (dominant)

- The easy-going buyer

- The skeptical buyer

***

1. **The indecisive buyer** is the type of buyer that sits on the fence. They will gather information and be too overwhelmed/nervous/concerned to make a definitive decision. Or they will lack the confidence in their decisions to make a comfortable one and to stick to it. With this buyer, you will take control and make the buying decision for them with an assumptive close.

An example of an assumptive close is as follows:
*C "All of your packages sound great. I really do not know which one to chose."

  **S "Based on what you have shared with me, (you can take this opportunity to reiterate) Option A is the best fit for you. We will get started today with a $200 down payment. I accept Visa, Mastercard and Amex through Stripe Merchant Services. Which card will you be using today?"

Legend
*C= Customer
**S= Sales Professional

No option to further confuse your buyer offered here. Close or BUST.

2. **The knowledgable buyer** is an educated consumer. If not handled properly the knowledgable buyer will overtake your sales conversation. You can lose control of your sale as they try to demonstrate that they know more about your product or service than you do. Be careful not to get into a war of words with them. Instead, compliment the buyer on their knowledge. (You can use this, along with a close-ended question, to regain control of the conversation if you lose the focus of your sales conversation.) You will offer this buyer a multiple choice closing. A multiple-choice closing gives the buyer the illusion that they have control of the sale. The truth is that a sale is a sale. However, having a decision to make will take your buyers attention off of trying to dominate your sales conversation.

An example of a multiple-choice close is as follows:
*C "I follow a lot of coaches so I know how you all think."

**S "Congrtulations for making the decision to follow professionals that can offer your value. Have you learned Anything of value?" (Notice the close-ended question)

Legend
*C= Customer
**S= Sales Professional

*C "Sure! have thought about my business a lot and learned a few things."

**S "I see that! Your dedication supported by the direction from a coach is a no-brainer. (Notice the challenge to their perception) You have the option to utilize OPTION 1, OPTION2 or OPTION 3 to serve your needs, however other smart buyers like you decided that OPTION 1 was best. And in my experience, (SME) I have learned that they are right."

*C "That one sounds good but I like OPTION 2 better."

**S "I can certainly see why you would. And I think that is a great start as well. (Setting up next sale) To get started today we will put $200 on a Visa, Mastercard or Amex. (Another choice) Which would you prefer to use? (Multiple choice and assumptive close)

3. **The easy-going buyer** is the buyer in no rush to buy. They are in no rush to solidify the deal and close the sale. As the sales professional, you will have to light a fire under your buyer's feet in order to make them uncomfortable. The skill you will use to do this is the creation of urgency. You can:

    A. Remind them of their pain point again. Draw a picture

Legend
*C= Customer
**S= Sales Professional

in their mind, that illustrates what happens if they do not act now.

B.   Remind them of their pain and make them overwhelmed with it so that they feel compelled to act now.

C.   Create pressure by helping your buyer recognize that you are offering a great deal......one that won't last. This will make them have to "act now" to take advantage of it.

An example of an urgent close is as follows:

*C "I know my business is not growing in they way that I want it to but I will get it right eventually."

**S "I remember the joy I heard in your voice as you spoke of having success in your business. How does it feel that you have not gotten there yet?"

*C "I am hopeful."

**S "I think getting some movement in the right direction will feel pretty good, right?" (Close-ended question)

*C "Yes."

Legend
*C= Customer
**S= Sales Professional

**S "I want to support you moving forward into the success that you knew you would have. I am offering you 10% off my services today as a reward for you finally taking control? To get started we will put $200 on a Visa, Mastercard or Amex. Which would you prefer to use?" (Urgent and Assumptive close)

4. **The skeptical buyer** is not sure that this is the right deal, the best deal, they do not trust you fully and/or are generally operating from a place of fear. In order to close this deal successfully, you will offer your buyer a summary close. As summary closing is one where you revisit the sale and restate what they escape by pulling the trigger. Remind them of how beneficial this is for them on the other side of the sale.

An example of a summary close is as follows:
*C "I am not sure that this is right for me."

**S "You spoke of having trouble losing sales consistently and making money. So, I offered you sales training to get the sales and money flowing for you and your business. And when you said you were nervous and didn't want to make a mistake, I understood you. I offered the most novice option so that you can get a feel for things before making an agreement on a premium package. And you know, I am here with you right?"

*C "Yes I know that."

Legend
*C= Customer
**S= Sales Professional

**S "Perfect. To get started we will put $200 on a Visa, Mastercard or Amex. Which would you prefer to use?" (Summary and assumptive close)

No matter which buyer you are working with, always remember to ask for the sale. Sales professionals often make this mistake...and it is a biggie.

Legend
*C= Customer
**S= Sales Professional

FINALIZING THE SALE

YOU DID IT! But the hard work is not over yet.

You tend to want to relax a bit after your buyer has said yes to your offer. What you may not realize is that you can lose a sale after it is made.   Enter buyer's remorse. That said, it is important to finalize the close of your sale in order to avoid losing it.

1. Gain agreement on the sale to ensure that you and your buyer are still on the same page. "Congratulations! Are you excited that you are moving towards more success?" (Notice the close-ended question)

2. Explain what to expect next in order to avoid your buyer feeling left out or forgotten in the next steps of this

process. People usually prefer knowing what to expect and what (if anything) is expected of them.

3. Make sure your buyer leaves with NO unanswered questions. Unanswered questions may come back to haunt you as they create buyer's remorse. Often times a buyer will say "I have no questions." However, they may think of something later. Probe to uncover any forgotten questions and leave it open for them to jump in the conversation should some arise. Be sure to invite them to connect with you should they come up with a question later as well. Make your buyer comfortable with your open availability.

4. Affirm your buyer's choices to do business with you with positive words of encouragement and empowerment. "I am proud of you and delighted that you took this first step."

5. Thank your new business partner for choosing you and for allowing you the opportunity to work with them. This shows that you appreciate and value your buyer. In return, the buyer will appreciate and value you too.

6. Ask for referrals. This step is the most forgotten. When you leave your buyer feeling good, asking for referrals is a smart business move. Your referring client will actually do a lot of the sales work for you. They will rave and share the wonderful experience they had with you. Closing the sale on a warm lead is much easier than closing the sale on a cold one.

CONCLUSION

SELLING PRODUCTS AND SERVICES is the lifeblood of your business.

Knowing how to sell and to close sales is part of the business behind your business if that makes sense. Learning how to navigate through closing sales conversations is one of those no-brainer steps. It is sometimes not only part of the business but the business itself. Your success or failure can depend on it. Mastering how to execute effective sales closings will be the engine underneath the hood of your business. This can make a tremendous difference in your confidence as well as in your bottom line. PRACTICE, PRACTICE and more PRACTICE to become a sales leader and to ensure that you close the deal.

ABOUT THE AUTHOR

Akia, a Bronx native and the product of a single parent household has not let the concrete jungle dim her light. She was an intelligent girl with an inquisitive mind anyway. As a teen, Akia acquired a ton of life lessons as an activist for the underserved and under-heard. Ironically, this is the same group she serves today. She went on to pursue a collegiate education at Wilmington University and studied Business Management and Information Technology. It was this education that laid the ground work for her entrepreneurial endeavors. Akia then went on to receive her coach training with The Coach Training Academy and received NLP training through the iNLP.

Throughout her professional career. Akia has held many titles including stock broker to high net worth clients near NYC's Wall Street and the esteemed position of Certified Financial Planner or CFP. She has worked for many well-known and respected companies including Citibank, JPMorgan, Apple, Google, and Microsoft. Today she is a very ambitious entrepreneur that has owned 6 + companies and acted in a business coaching and on a consulting basis for 4 others. These unique experiences have helped shape

Akia into the dynamic powerful and inspirational woman she is today.

Her business, Optimize Your Spark was officially born in 2015 after unofficially coaching many businesses since 2001. Akia now serves as a Certified Life Coach and supports women, people of color and members of the LGBT community that own businesses. She coaches and consults her clients through branding, social media marketing, email marketing, building packages, package pricing, budgeting, target markets, target audiences, confident sales conversations, broadening their networks and more. As a Certified Master NLP Practitioner Akia also does work on mindset using various modalities and submodalities in an effort to help her clients get out of their own way allowing them to court and achieve success. Akia is also a member of the well-respected Certified Coaches Alliance as well as the International Coach Federation. Her business operates under the ethical guidelines and moral standards set by both allowing her clients ease, confidence, and trust in their coaching partnerships. She is also a Public Speaker, club President of her Toastmasters, Club President of CEO Space New York and North East and a Huffington Post Contributor.

Check her out:
www.AkiaTaylor.com
https://www.FACEBOOK.com/optimizeyourspark/
https://www.TWITTER.com/akiabrooke/
https://www.INSTAGRAM.com/akiabrooke/
https://www.LINKEDIN.com/in/akiataylor

Thanks for reading!

Please add a short review on Amazon.

Let me know what you thought.

If you are still not as confident as you would like to be and want to expand upon the basics that I shared with you here Optimize Your Sales Closings Learning Track will get you there. In addition to acquiring more refined sales skills, you will enjoy an NLP sales training that will certify you in NLP and ensure that you get the sale.

Online marketing support genius is available. Spark Your Marketing online course and learning track will help you to become more visible so that your dream clients can invest in your offers.

Customized support 1:1 coaching with Certified Business Coach Akia Taylor is available.

If this book was useful for you, why not share it with your friends?

Optimize Your Spark
Turn Your Spark into an Inferno
Akia Taylor

Dear Lovely,

Did you know that there is an art to skillful selling?

There is a selling technique called the consultative sale that makes selling ideas feel like a regular ole' conversation. And even though it FEELS like a regular old conversation it is one that requires a little skill on your part.

What THIS BOOK will do for you and your closings:

1. You will experience a boost in your confidence. You can have conversations with a PURPOSE and not bomb right before you get the dollars in your hand. (clients are like sharks and can smell fear a mile away)

2. Teach you to overcome objections with skill and ease.

3. Learn how to close each type of customer and have THEM thank YOU for the sale. (yes, they will thank you)

A sale only happens when there is a need to be filled. Think of the sale as a service...cuz...that's what it is. And also be knowledgeable about HOW to do it.

We are playing BIG. And learning how to do it right is what people who play big do.

XOXOXOXO

Akia Taylor

www.ingramcontent.com/pod-product-compliance
Lightning Source LLC
Chambersburg PA
CBHW061207180526
45170CB00002B/995